4/17/13

Sharon,

Enjoy.

P. Kocak

TIPP HILL LITANIES

Celebrating a Syracuse Heritage

PAUL KOCAK

Kocak Wordsmiths Ink
347 Whittier Avenue
Syracuse, NY 13204

ISBN-13: 978-0615774534
ISBN-10: 0615774539

Cover photo and author photo:
Adrianna B. Kocak

Imprint logo:
leonard assante :: assante design inc.

Cover design, interior design, and layout:
Becky's Graphic Design
www.beckysgraphicdesign.com

To Peter Coleman,
Janice McKenna, and Pat Hogan,
pillars among many

PROLOGUE

How hard it is to escape from places. However carefully one goes they hold you – you leave little bits of yourself fluttering on the fences – like rags and shreds of your very life.
— *Katherine Mansfield*

I would be in exile now but everywhere's the same. — *Phil Ochs*

No place is a place until things that have happened in it are re-membered in history, ballads, yarns, legends, or monuments. Fic-tions serve as well as facts. — *Wallace Stegner*

This is not a history of the Tipperary Hill neighborhood in Syracuse, New York. At least it is not a history in the typical sense of chronologies and facts and narrative. Rather, this is a history insofar as poetry captures the narrative of our inner lives, the weave of the strands of time and person and place. In that sense, this is a personal history of a neighborhood and its people as well as a make-believe speculation on Tipp Hill's past, present, and future.

You will not find here all the names and fables that history has recorded concerning Tipperary Hill. Nor will you find either a roster of resentments or a retelling of the elders' tales. There are faint echoes of that, but it would be fraudulent for a "newcomer" such as I am (1994) to engage in such serious, or humorous, matters.

This is not so much about the facts as about the spirit of Tipp Hill. I offer an exploration of what makes any neighborhood a relevant place in a 21st-century America often characterized by a sterile sameness scrubbed of history. In doing so, I sometimes stray from the boundaries of what is considered Tipp Hill in order to provide a context, a contrast, or a texture.

And there are surprises here, too. I purposely broadened the postcard picture of Irish-American Tipp Hill to include Americans of Ukrainian, Polish, German, Croatian, Italian, Slovak, and other backgrounds.

What does make a place? Collective memory, cultural heritage, communal purpose — surely these are some of the necessary ingredients. For me, Tipp Hill's sense of place is conducive to poetry (or poetic prose) because it draws on stories and collective memories that speak of loss, exile, community, and pride. Poetry is the perfect medium for such messages, for it elicits song and melody, both sad and joyous and profound and whimsical. You will also see liturgical and other religious references, because they are part of my personal vernacular.

I invite you to sample one man's take on an endearing and enduring place. If I have summoned the spirit of Tipperary Hill for you, just a little bit, then I am grateful.

Paul Kocak
Tipperary Hill, Syracuse, N.Y.
February 25, 2013

Tipp Hill Litanies

READY SET
SHAMROCK RUN

for Marty Masterpole and his band of merry volunteers

Arched and eager

calves and thighs

panting human thoroughbreds

steaming in the crisp March air

thousands poised and posed

taut with fervor

melting snow

festive air

emerald balloons

Norman Rockwell throngs on sidewalks

welcoming this moment

charged with pride

win or lose

LITANY FOR ROSAMOND GIFFORD ZOO

for Ethan

For golden lion tamarins,
O salutaris hostia.

With two-toed sloth and blue-tongued skink,
Miserére nobis.

To barred tiger salamander and leopard gecko,
Asperges me, Dómine.

Lo, laughing kookaburra and palawan peacock
pheasant, *Kyrie, eléison.*

For queen angelfish and Madagascar hissing
cockroach, *Ora pro nobis.*

With naked mole rat and Egyptian fruit bat,
Christe, exáudi nos.

To guanaco and roseate spoonbill,
Orate pro nobis.

Lo, LaMancha goat and axolotl,
Te rogamus, audi nos.

From Amur tiger and spectacled bear,
Parce nobis, Dómine.

With Eastern hellbender and desert chuckwalla,
Et cum spíritu tuo.

With radiated tortoise and reticulated python,
Et clamor meus ad te véniat.

Vos omnes sancta animalia,
Ut fructus terræ dare et conservare dignéris.

All you holy animals,
That it may please you to give and preserve to our
use the kindly fruits of the earth.

Amen.

ODE TO THE
Onion Domes

If not blinded by snow or sun

you will see

just past the declaration

NOW THAT WE ARE HERE

NOWHERE ELSE MATTERS

painted blue over yellow

Ukrainian colors

on a field of coal black

on the railroad bridge

over West Fayette

on the horizon

five emerald onion domes

sitting atop

the gateway

to Tipperary Hill

five beckoning beauties

sentinels and greeters

iconic landmark

St. John the Baptist Ukrainian Catholic Church

from 1913, year of my Slovak father's birth

anointing our eyes

christening our field of vision

from Lodi Street a lighted summons

bathed in nighttime glow

celebrating

Celtic tribes and Slavic clans

and stray stragglers from Destiny

Canticle of the Stone Throwers

green over red

world upside down

red under green

take that

defiance as honor

color as code

rocks as words

take that

stop me if you can

broken glass for broken lands

jagged stone from solid heart

take that

toil and grit

worn on sleeve

raveled by rage

take that

green over red

grief unkenneled

ancient keening

take that

from Upperchurch to Thurles in Tipperary

from this Hill

to the shores of silk or sin

take that take this take us

Burnet Park Litany

At the sentinel saplings

shower us with sainthood

"in loving memory of Suzanne E. Forth"

silence us with mercy

for these rolling Irish-ish hills

have mercy on our eyes

for golfers' lost and wailing balls

may the scores be false and farcical

from the dogshit-riddled path

may our feckin' feet free us

at the cityscape vesper dusk

may the robin sing its breast red

down Bill O'Leary Drive

may you skate on confetti blossoms

from the roaring of the zoo-caged lions

may the den of inequity save you

and in the fold of yarding deer

hear us, o antlers, hear us

Life, The Serial

On my misty, coolish dogwalk, I noticed that the
graffito of LIFE with the "i" dotted with an "x,"
on a small electrical utility shed, was gone.

LIFE, vanished, without a trace.

As if LIFE were but a dream.

I miss LIFE.

Where'd it go, now that its resident surface is
scrubbed clean, freshly painted, pristine?

Can LIFE even exist on such a sanitized surface?

LIFE, I was just getting to know you. I was on the
cusp of what you wanted to tell me, who put you
there, and why.

Now, it's like starting over.

FRAGMENTS FROM
'THE BOOK OF SACRED NAMES'

From Gooley and Gilmartin
To Paddon and Prybyla
praise and remembrance.

Hark, merry multitudes of Masterpole, Maione,
Mazuryk, Maher, Moriarity, Moynihan,
McAndrew, McKenna. And Mykolajewycz,
Maroney, McCormick, Murphy, Moore.
More? Here is Murray, McGuire, Moran, Macko,
Marko, Mosher, McGroarty, Mullane, McGadey,
McEneny, Malick, Mulholland, McCarthy, Maslak,
Mishansky, Maliwesky, Maliarchuk. And Moffett,
Mead, McNamara, Mooney, Merenkiw, Mulder.

O neighborly nicknames of Bocko and Eggo and
Groucho, Bushel and Buzzard and Bullets,
Soup Head and Saucer Eye,
Dassy and Pug,
Special and Medium and Timahawk, Elder, and

Tinty Tim.
Ye Dinny and Dinty and Wig and Neddy Two
Blocks and Goddamn Man.
Hail Holy Mary and Huckle and Shoddy-Wa-Wa.
O Cranky, Cookie, Shang, Common Man,
Bayonet, and Bounce.
Ye Pious Kate and Nibsy and Ned and Sean-a-Feg!

Praise streetwise wordsmiths Coleridge, Emerson,
Milton, Tennyson
And poets Bryant, Whittier, and Lowell
As well as nameless others known and unknown,
past and future.

A tip of the Tipp brim to Brereton, Bradshaw,
Bergin, Barry, and Britt, Butler, Busko, Burke,
Bagan, Boyson, Bannon, Brown,
And Bubnack, Batcho, Buranich, Burnet O indeed
Burnet.

Roseate garlands to Geddes, Gleason, Galvin,
Griffin, Gross, Gallati, Ganz, Gilbert, Gorman,
Ganley, Gridley, and Guerdet.

Ahoy, Anderson, Ahern, Amaya, Artymovych, and
Abbott.

Pray for us, Saints Patrick, John the Baptist, Peter,

Paul, Brigid, Joseph, Mark the Evangelist — and
All Saints; we need your help.

Dozens of hurrahs and gratitude to DeGuglielmo,
Dawson, Dravek, Donovan, DiOrio, Dugan,
Driscoll, Dankow, Danko, Dydyk, Dorsey, Dwyer,
Ducar, Dosyak, Davis, Doyle, Dowd, Dillon,
Dottolo, Downes, and Dooher.

Lo, rich reveries of Ryfun, Ryan O Ryans, Rybak,
Roesch, Robinson, Rowe, Reddy, Reale, Roche,
Rolfe, Rendziek, Roik, and Reagan.

Cradles of Corbett, Costello, Conroy, Carroll,
Coleman, Coman, Chupeck, Cook, Crough,
Covey, Casey, Callahan, Cummings, Curcio, and
Curr.

Not to unmention Nowakowski, Nossett, Nozynski,
Norris, Nodzo, Naughton, Fenlon, Fisher, Fahey,
Fabisiak, Folley, Towe, Trach, Thomas, Taylor,
Ludden, Laird, Locke, Leise, Losty, Ewndziek, and
Eisenberg.

Say yes to Spath, Sturick, Starmer, Stamm, Schultz,
Slowiatycki, Smoral, Schmitt, Schmidt, Shannahan,
Shanahan, Stringham, Slattery, Stapleton, Satalin,
Solomon, Sheremeta, Sopchak, Starushak, Swete,

Schuyler, and Strodel.

Oh me oh my O'Sullivan, O'Riley, O'Connor, and Oberst.

Okay and more to Kernan, Kohanski, Kennedy, Kallfelz, Kastler, Kowaleski, Kwiatkowski, Keller, Kocak, Kicak, Klug, Koczan, Kudlick, Komar, Konutiak, Kalenak, Kurylo, Kusnir, Kelly, and Kamenecky.

Hello, goodbye, hello to Hartnett, Harrington, Hazard, Hourigan, Harrison, Harasym, Halligan, Hallinan, Husak, Hnotko, Hayduke, Hrynyk, Houston, Hanley, and Hayes.

Pause or parade with Pysnack, Parashak, Petruniak, Peltz, Pinkasewicz, Piso, Pritchard, Powers, and Piedmonte.

Walk arm and arm with the likes of Welsh, Walsh, Whalen, Walker, Williams, Welychorsky, Woryan, Wright, Waite, Waurek, Wachna, and Warguleski.

Adieu, goodday, and goodnight to Underwood, Young, Zipprich, Zacholl, Vassallo, and Valley.

And now it is time to turn the page.

Tipp Hill Streets: Poets' Collage

John Greenleaf Whittier: *"All is not lost. The angel of God's blessing Encamps with Freedom on the field of fight."*

Samuel Taylor Coleridge: *"The frost performs its secret ministry, Unhelped by any wind."*

James Russell Lowell: *"May is a pious fraud of the almanac. A ghastly parody of real Spring."*

William Cullen Bryant: *"All that tread The globe are but a handful to the tribes That slumber in its bosom."*

Lord Alfred Tennyson: *"Though much is taken, much abides; and though We are not now that strength which in old days Moved earth and heaven, that which we are, we are."*

Ralph Waldo Emerson: *"The mad wind's night-work, The frolic architecture of the snow."*

John Milton: *"They also serve who only stand and wait."*

Litany to Some Merchants Past – and Present

From Hennigan's Silver Star Grocery and
Shanahan's too, *a peach and some beef and a candy
for the kids.*

To Groucho Hewitt's Fish Fry and Casey's Fish
Market, *scales and scales and Lenten sales.*

For Brigandi's Tailors and Isadore Wichman,
a stitch in time and eternity.

At Callahan-Hanley Mooney, Ryan, Tindall, and
Macko-Vassallo funeral homes, *a lap around the
beads and Godspeed to ya.*

From the James Kernan Theater,
song and dance and the clapping of hands.

At Corbett's Hardware Store,
nuts and bolts and pipes and sawdust.

For O'Riley's Ice Cream Parlor, Oompa's, and the
Brooklyn Pickle, *never a melting of delicious flavors
nor the bread go stale.*

To the Shamrock Grill and Stone Throwers Cafe,
a pint raised in pride and no trouble now, boys.

From Ralph DeGuglielmo's Shoe Repair and
Cookie Caloia's, *handy feats for feet to be feted, and
a kind road a-rising.*

From O'Brien's Pharmacy and Niki's Quick Cup,
a cure for the common cold out there.

To F.J. Manton's, Sam's Market, Brilbeck's, and
Byrne Dairy, *some bread, my household for some
bread; or milk and a scratchie.*

To MacVicker's Machine Shop,
the grinding of our fears amid our daily gears.

At Coleman's, Nibsy's, Blarney Stone, Steve's,
Wheeler's, Rosie's, McAvan's, O'Dea's, the Gass
Pump, and more, *some cures for what ales you.*

And from Cashel House, *may the light stay green on
top and you be blessed with a driveway.*

Nowhereland, Just North of Somewhere

Steps in Syracuse snowswept

Say it slower now

(Why the freezing weeping?)

Twin tracks tundra

Bridged rusted aborted

West Fayette Street spanned spun spawned

To what end

Nowhere

Somewhere

Over there by Fowler

No trains a-comin'

No whistle blowin'

In the wind or sun or rain

Unless you listen

Have you seen it lived it

Off the map off the grid

Derailed

WEST SIDE
RECESSIONAL

Remember the recession

in Fairmount a downturn

in back of Holy Family

a grotto whose cobbled inner recesses

reveal a Virgin Mary

Remember that recession

at Burnet Park with upturns and swerves

emeralding in April chill

sporting robins and purple finches

and flinches in the recesses of golfers

Remember a recession

on Tipperary Hill

caught in the eyes of Mike

all-season bottle man

asking for nothing, five cents at a time

JURY DUTY

Subzero. I decided to walk, let the roaring light bleach

The testimony spinning in my head, steaming

Traffic on West Fayette, the five emerald onion domes

Of the Ukrainian church on Tipp Hill at my back, going to trial.

Murder. Manslaughter. Death (funny, I can't for the life of me see the man's Laughter in that word today) by the blade hotter than August beaches, They said. He said. She said. All together now.

Me, I'd like a revelation, if you please, here
A notarized transcript of verifiable fact, there.
Something neon and sure; true

To the taste of metal in the blood, say.

"Voir dire," someone said. Indeed,

What do *you* say, sparrow on the barbed wire?

I didn't quite catch it, not even a beaky breath?
(Though I snatched a frozen glance from your
pellet eye as you flickered away.)

What can you tell me? I need a sign

But instead you rudely leave me to the snowy
silence in my chest

And the bells, the shifting gears, the fumes, the
crunch of the boot.

ORCHARD

to walk amid the aisles

cathedral crispness

a ladder

branches with baubles

red and reddening

green and yellowing

beckoning bites

to reach up Edenward

Macouns Cortlands

Honey Crisps Macintoshes

galas of Galas

sampling the goods

bursting with appleness

stepping amid rot

mushy decadence

ripe for the picking

how can this be

reach even

overreach

arch

blessed fruit

of the womb of this golden Saturday

the miracle of the moment

now is the time

see

grab

bite

taste

chew

swallow

smile

sigh

amid the boughs

a long way from Tipperary

To Touch Rice

In the centuries-old tradition of sushi apprenticeship, years must pass before one can "touch rice." Those wishing to learn to master sushi must spend years watching and observing.

To touch baseball

To hold pen

To tap keys

To pull trigger

To teach student

To hold chalk

To diagram sentence

To touch heart

To say prayer

To ring bells

To roast coffee

To taste tea

To smell honey

To eat locusts

THE EYES HAVE IT

you can feel the metallic cold boring in on you

or the sportive romping with Amaryllis in the shade

molten rage

dull resolve

sadness unto death

it's all in the eyes isn't it

dancing or drowning

flying or flat

the eyes have it

from County Tipperary

to this arid alien shore

THE SUBJUNCTIVE OF EPIPHANY EVE

Were the subjunctive to speak

I doubt that

Would they

If molecular biology

Were kings to fly

Or stars to speak

Contingent desire

Breathy

Breathless

Is more

Is just plain everything

As in this daily epiphany

The bread (crumbs) of life

Ordinary

As my morning toast

Luscious in butter

And tea

For too

Too much

The View From Here

At the crest of the back of the zoo
brood over a sun-drenched city
meandering homeward
bound for danger or play
angles skewed off the grid
Niagara Mohawk's stately art
deco rated a skyline
a Dome now an ancient
artifact of a former space age
alien architecture before
digital meant other than fingers
of light fast fading
contrails of commerce.

Above the greens above the fairways
a House of Providence
once for orphans
now the sirens wailing
Wegmans lost apostrophe
Bellevue, yes, literally
sweeping up Velasko's vista
country club miles
even decades from Corcoran

taillights of today's
flight into exurbia
escaping the harsh glare
and beauty of ordinary rainbows.

And down there
the pool empty
or thrashing
cobalt or cold
gated and garrulous
seasonal to the core.

The silence of the missing
aircraft days
after 9/11
the bats zigzagging
searching for darkness.

Looking east
another land
a farther field
do they ever look
over here?

It Was in the Mills, It Was

We rolled our sleeves
gnarled our hands and
sweat our bones to dust

We lost our brothers, fathers, and sons
husbands married to the mill
making ends meet
a mockery to the the grammar
of need the algebra of want

It was in the mills, it was
we made a buck, brought home bread
soup to some and swooned to sleep

It was on the canal, it was
camaraderie and clawing
earth for progress
barging into the future

Sanderson Geddes Solvay Process Oberdorfer
Terra Cotta Works Iroquois China Onondaga Pottery
Frazer & Jones Franklin Syracuse Iron Works
Onondaga too
salt in the wounds brine in the eyes
fire in the belly
Irish Pole Slovak
and every working man
sleeves rolled up
dawn to dusk
in the mines of manufacturing

It was in the mills, it was
we made a living
we carved a life
we found a place

It was in the mills, it was
we lost our jobs
we lost our way, we did

and wonder where tomorrow goes
with archives of tinted photos
yellowed pages
grandfathered clauses
suburban flight
divorced from opportunity

servile service jobs
menial madness

it was in the mills, it was
supposed to last forever
it was

LITANY OF PASS ARBORETUM

From the dogged detritus dotting our path,
save our soles.

For the nomenclature of stately trees,
praise be thy Latin mysteries.

To the view of gravestones and myrtle,
may your eyes melt with memory.

At the hillock of music and frolic,
may our folk be shamrocked and Séamused.

In the vintage of autumn,
may your palette be timbred.

Through your black wrought iron gate,
pass the eye of a penitent camel.

And in the dawning of springtime,
let your sprouting spawn robins.

Hymn to Lake Effect

Windswept, from where or when who knows
light's verge

the other side of arid
snow

moist to moisture, lash to lashes, spindrift spun,
moody madness, baleful blizzard

Cause and effect, lake and effect, rippling
raptures of featherweight

showered by Ontario's halo
of lacustrine lustre

dust upon dust upon swirl upon crystal upon flake
upon hill and plain and dale and Onondaga gone
gaga granting

honeycombs of alabaster
silence

Mowing the Last Lawn

After this time maybe I'll put the mower in the basement

This hand-operated machine which I chose not for any benevolent reason

The previous one always stalled and sputtered the hell with it

To sit down there all winter

Among dried ordure and braided grass

Catshit and hairballs, a dead toilet

Goggle-eyed toys and aquariums and art project monsters

And a living washing machine and dryer

This Saturday it is almost too hot, me with my panama hat

I'm not doing this with the anger I see and hear
and smell on most Saturdays

The suburban armies of the noon fighting off their
decay

With a vengeance

I leave a clovery patch in the corner by the
graveyard of drooped sunflowers

Spent and seeded and looking downright sad
about it

Just to leave something undone

I like the sound of the cuttings their spin

The weavery of it

The back of the lot hardly has grass at all dead
leaves and twigs

I yell over to Joe working on his porch

How I'm sick and tired of stepping in dog shit for
the fourth time

Well you do have a dog, he says

And I don't know if he is scolding me or being
neighborly

The vines on the back rusted fence the color of
orange skins left in an oven

I don't want to know the names of every leaf

Just the secret fire that erupted from the green
veins

My own fire never was too secret was it

They saw it from a mile away and ran for the hills

Look at those drunken hedges raucous since I cut
them in

What June when I cut the cord once again and
tried to see if I could

Snip the chain-link fence while being electrocuted

I'll let the hedges stay unruly till the spring

Like the hair my father railed against and took as

a personal insult

Did it matter at all, now, Dad

If I made it this far and farther

Those wasps whose nests I sprayed and swatted
and crushed back in May

Was that the way to go?

I wonder where they're hiding now

What silent heat to keep them through an infinite
Syracuse December

While taunting me even laughing some call it
buzzing

The stubborn back lawn one more time.

Meditation on a Leaf

a pale yellow of exquisite blond reduction: light straw dusted by sand; shield-shaped, serrated edges coming to a pointy crest at the top, two inches top to bottom not counting the stem; an inch across, if that; a network of veins mapping roads to nowhere or everywhere or anywhere; rusty freckles of decay ringed like a constellation in dusk drenched in desert tones; the first signs of curling along the outer edges, a natural rigor mortis; the single solitary leaf poses for me as I sit in my car; a nude model; I stare at it as it sits in repose on my windshield; I resist the temptation to turn on the wiper; blade; I resist the urge to flick it off; arrested; the tiniest breath-breeze flickers the stubborn leaf, making it waver and waggle; a dry amber flame in daylight; don't leave me; let go; stay; let go; turning over a new leaf; not turning over an old leaf; gone when I return to the car; forgotten, except for a smaller leafy cousin, caught in a crack; waiting; waiting

Nightwalk

Walked blind for a while there

Letting the dog see my eyes

Closed for R&R (rest and repair)

Feeling the gravel as much as hearing

That bat swoop nightward

Dwarfing the traffic growl on Avery Avenue

What nerve those summers I worked with blind
kids

Pretending I knew their ways

Eating night in monastic rooms

Tonight interrupted by outlaw golfers

Playing the green in youth's faithful madness

Stealing glee from the jaws of the coyote chorus

Sirening in their municipal asylum

Or merely partying Friday night

As beams from a skybound plane

Single me out wincing wonder

December Night's Walk One-Sentence Meditation

On a still, snow-crunching night with bright Orion's Belt *(Three Kings or Three Sisters or Three Nothings or Three Anythings, take your pick)* guiding us, the dog and I walked Burnet Park and its islands of nightshade green, its light show dotting the Happy Holidays *(Unnamed)* landscape of snow and ice and memories of June, both of us delighting in the jingly-jangly clip-clop clop-clip symphony of horse hooves, children's voices, and five ladies with Slavic accents in a cigarette-smoke-wreathed circle bidding us good evening.

DEWATERING HOLE

As I strolled through Burnet Park this evening, I was greeted by the shock of emptiness, an alabaster rectangular hole with black crosses painted at the far end. The pool was empty. Stark empty! On August 19! No lifeguards? (Back at college?) No cash? Where did all the turquoise madness drain to? And what did all the kids do as they approached the railings only to find this stark absence of cerulean-emerald shimmering in the heat?

Empty. Gone.

And summer, rudely hanging around, sweating.

REVELATION

the detritus of winter rising up like pacific atolls
volcanic garbage not even a rousing rain can wash
away can clean cleanse as in a rite of absolution
ego te absolvo the melted snows dribble down
the hill tipperary hill and you get surprised seeing
anything a squashed plastic bottle invitations
to subscribe the head of a child's smiling stuffed
pal a flattened pancake fabric why the smile the
vacant stare along with beer cans and bottle caps
and runaway trash can covers branches leaves all
tawny almost colorless so monochrome yet hints
hums whispers tuneups throat clearings of melody
harmony infinite pantone matching scales of vernal
vehemence

HAIKU AND OTHER SHORT GIVE-AND-TAKES

nightsnow crunch footsteps

silent flakes falling freely

white upon silver

soft wind in the pines

garlands lighting Burnet Park

festival of bright

forsythia rage

asleep under April snow

the steaming pavement

last October's leaves

alabaster chilled veneer

lazy flurries fall

rolling emerald

sonorous robin's lament

dusky cumulus

old friend chicory

back for August blues

the moon at noon

clouds fracture crescent sliver

St. Houdini's Eve

ashes of my cigar

albino Vatican-like smokestack plumes

my nostrils frost-thrilled

green-to-amber-to-red up on university hill

six sparrows soaring

copper patina St. John's domes

echoing vespers

starlings bickering on maples

Jackson Pollock stratocumulus

the twig snaps under my boot

peach lightning, fluorescent snow

a herd of deer turns and runs

this is Valentine's Day?

a lone robin's vespers

the moon climbs above the pines

the dog walks me

in the rearview mirror

her blazing sunglasses, neon hair

— the light turns green

honey locust feast

autumnal ginkgo showers

fans splayed silently

front lawn tulip leaves

sloping to downhill sidewalk

corabell spits fire

scimitar moonlight

Maxfield Parrish skyview

zigzag bat brushstrokes

too ravaged to play

you sit, mentoring me

grip, watch, bend, swing

SEEDSTORM

Looks like Onan had some kind of field day. The ground at Burnet Park cleared and grubbed, scraped raw. Where the sumac and brush were. Stripped bare. But down toward the corner of Coleridge *(yes, we also have Tennyson, Tompkins, Lowell, and other streets so eponymously named)* evergreens were planted with stakes and wires to keep them straight. But back to Onan and his field day. Seed spread like a storm. A swirl of grass seed scattered over the freshened land. A feast of fecundity in waiting. Like insulation blown in. Teal paint. Snowdrift. Seeds. Seeds. Seeds spilled hurled thrown cast broad over the naked earth. The spilling of the seed as if in some kind of helter-skelter rampage, even splashed up against the bark of pines. Seed that does not look like seed but rather some cellular fabric dried snot greenish blue carpet. The seeds sleep. And wait. To whom will it matter if and when this protean blizzard ends up as dog-shit-riddled lawn, eye-catching landscape, dandelion heaven, or emerald Eire lookalike?

LİFE

continued

I've told you before of the graffito **LIFE** in Burnet Park, once there, then gone, scrubbed, scoured, painted over.

I saw **LIFE** again yesterday.

LIFE moved *(to at least two places)* over on Hiawatha Boulevard, Syracuse, not far from the imagined world of Destiny USA. Emblazoned in uppercase letters amid industrial debris and abandon.

I was grateful to see some **LIFE** yesterday. It gave me some hope.

Today I imagine **LIFE** was there, a little elusive, shrouded in twilight, but I did not see it directly.

I was cast into twilight. I am bathed in twilight.

I am living in a zone of twilight.

But **LIFE** awaits. . . as a statement, a fact, not merely posed as a question.

LIGHTS ALIVE

Entering Burnet Park, at the top of Syracuse's
Tipperary Hill, I noticed the presence of absence.

Missing were the strings of festive amberish-
whitish lights draping several mature trees. More
accurately, on closer inspection, many of these
strings of lights remained on the trees but were
unplugged, unlit. To paraphrase Hemingway, a
clean, unlighted place. Darker, moodier in the
night wind.

Higher up the winding drive, gone was the
banner of lights, high up between two tall trees,
announcing HAPPY HOLIDAYS, demurely
(or cowardly) declining to declare exactly which
holidays, as if the secular gods would gripe about
the explicit nomenclature of the God-incarnate In
Nomine Patris feast.

Some lights still shone.

Within the gates of the pool, an image of a toy
train illuminated the space between two lifeguard
stations, tall seats, sentinels overlooking a white

and snowless empty pool, bereft of the excited
jeering and obscenity and glee *(mostly in Spanish)*
of its frolicking residents.

Back near the zoo, some trees or streetlights had,
what?, snowmen or holly or candy canes brightly
shining.

Sirens in the distance got the coyotes or wolves
stirred up at the zoo, singing their own eerie siren
songs.

In the distance, downtown, the Niagara Mohawk
building *(I'll never call it the NationalGrid
building)* and M&T Bank were wrapped in lights
of green.

Spotting a skateboarder, with shorts on, passing
me, I circled back to monitor him, wondering if
that was a spray can in his hand.

Did he paint the now-gone **LIFE** graffito?

The echoes of his skateboard antics forced me
to conclude, no, for now, he was too busy just
skating along, skimming the surface, riding the
landward wave.

E L E V E N

More than one and one

But standing aligned

Sometimes askew

The path bedecked with branch and leaf

Maple, redbud, oak, and beech

And worn with steps we've trod

From Tipperary to Connemara

On rocky cliffs and silver strands

Here's to us

and many more.

SПOW
МARCH

blind white particulate crystalline settling

aftermath do the numbers

paths buried cars hidden ground missing depth

guessing wonders

chunk block rock tock tick smack snow snew

sown strown strewn

alabaster albino vanilla creamy lumen beachtide

flake wake

ADIEU ST. MARK'S, HELLO PORTER

Father Joe Bergin's farewell

"the God of surprises"

not dimming eye fire

nor hardwood clacking

of fierce Irish stepdancers

coffee brewing on Tuesday nights

in fellowship of failure

redemption's first step

Porter School kids

fanning out under flags

of nations and need

the magnet of success

an article of faith

iron filings

awaiting array and form

20 iNTERROGASTORiES

1. How would you like to die?

2. What is it like to be alive?

3. Where would you want to sing?

4. Why do you want to know?

5. Whom will you embrace as the sky is rent?

6. Has the Burnet Park burnt sienna cooled?

7. Do the words echo in your veins?

8. Have you questioned having?

9. Am I blue (a muted cobalt just south of Antwerp)?

10. Would you if you could without getting caught or punished?

11. With whom will you dive, sail, skim, [note serial comma] or float?

12. Against what odds or flesh will you melt?

13. Who remembers that nameless electric thrill?

14. If not here and now, where and when?

15. Should there be a law, any law?

16. That being said, what is silence?

17. Could the waves just stop?

18. Which color will you wear and what language will ban it?

19. Is keeping score against the rules?

20. In the end, can you call it a day or something else, i.e., some unit of time or space or imagination or pendulum-swinging suggestion or somnambulism?

iF ПOt FOR TiPPERARY

If they came from Galway or Connemara
would the taxonomy of eponymy
give birth to variations of derivation?

If they arrived more from Malahide or Donegal
would we celebrate a Celtic pride
with other monikers for hilly terrain?

And what of the Onondagas, of the Haudenosaunee,
with clans of wolf, turtle, beaver, snipe, heron, deer,
eel, bear, or hawk?

Alas they came from Lemkivschyna and Halychna
Ukrainians uprooted
but we do not call it Lemkos Hill.

And so it is Tipperary Hill
a pinnacle of pride
a spire of survival.

What of tomorrow and decades hence
as the tapestry of America adds threads and strands:

shall we keep the name through snow and sun?
shall we etch in stone what words have wrought?

Appendix

Here are English translations for the Latin invocations in "Litany for Rosamond Gifford Zoo."

O salutaris hostia. O saving host.

Miserére nobis. Have mercy upon us.

Asperges me, Dómine. Sprinkle me, Lord.

Kyrie, eléison. Lord, have mercy.

Ora pro nobis. Pray for us.

Christe, exáudi nos. O Christ, graciously hear us.

Orate pro nobis. Pray for us.

Te rogamus, audi nos. We beseech you to hear us.

Parce nobis, Dómine. Spare us, Lord.

Et cum spíritu tuo. And with your spirit.

Et clamor meus ad te véniat. And let my cry come unto you.

Vos omnes sancta animalia, All you holy animals,

Ut fructus terræ dare et conservare dignéris. That it may please you to give and preserve to our use the kindly fruits of the earth.

NOTE ON SOURCES
ACKNOWLEDGMENTS

Although this is not a document of history, history and its artifacts are ever present. I am indebted to several invaluable resources. The online archives of The (Syracuse) Post-Standard via **Syracuse. com** served as a well of information and inspiration. In particular, a long piece on Tipperary Hill by John Francis McCarthy taught me much and gave me ideas for poems. Similarly, several columns by Sean Kirst of The Post-Standard shed light on people, events, and history — and planted seeds for poems or prose. Gregg Tripoli and the fine folks at the Onondaga Historical Association opened their doors and let me enter other eras of rich Syracuse history. The online archives of St. John the Baptist Ukrainian Catholic Church yielded a treasure of names and reflections of pride. Other church-related websites provided similar stories. The stone World War II memorial that stands at the park entrance by Burnet Park Drive and Coleridge Avenue has given me pause often. I hope I have faithfully recorded all the names remembered there. Finally, thanks to all the locals or would-be locals who have shared their stories and remembrances, usually with a twinkle of the eye and a laugh. I regret any omissions of notable people, events, or what-have-you. No slight is intended. I must report I spurned offers of a long cup of coffee or tea to hear colorful tales of Tipperary Hill. The reason is simple: the central voice here is mine. Alas, you will have to write your own book to capture other voices. There's plenty of room for more Tipp Hill books on the shelf, or in your e-reader, is there not?

Made in the USA
Charleston, SC
02 April 2013